£4.50

Hi...

Is it that time again? Has a year gone by already? Ok, then here we go.....

Hi! We'd like to welcome all of our tour friends and fans to the pages of this our second annual.

You know, it really is hard to believe that a whole year has gone by. It's been even more hectic than last year, with extensive tours of the USA and Europe under our belts, so now we're having a break and whilst you are reading this we'll probably be lying in the sun somewhere doing absolutely nothing.

Sometimes people ask us if we get tired of touring. The honest answer to that is "yes, of course we get tired". With such a demanding schedule, who wouldn't? But we never tire of actually touring. You see, we get to meet so many of our friends that it makes all of the effort worthwhile. For instance, we've just completed a tour of Europe and the UK and we saw so many faces that we recognised from the last time.

It really is gratifying to know that you are out there rootin' for us and that you are really into the ideals we are trying to achieve. No words can express our thanks to you for your continuing and ever growing support. We love you all and we're going to be coming back to see you again real soon. Until then,
.......................THANK YOU!

NEW KIDS ON THE BLOCK™

5	...HELLO – WE'RE BACK AGAIN
8	...NEW KIDS OVER EUROPE 1991
16	...FACT FILE ON JORDAN
18	...NEW KIDS .. IN THEIR OWN WORDS
20	...NEW KIDS SCRAPBOOK 1
22	...FACTFILE ON DANNY
26	...EVERYTHING YOU EVER WANTED TO KNOW ...
28	...QUIZ PAGE AND WORD SEARCH
31	...SCRAPBOOK 2
32	...FACTFILE ON JONATHAN
34	...SCRAPBOOK 3
35	...JORDAN PROFILE
36	...DONNIE PROFILE

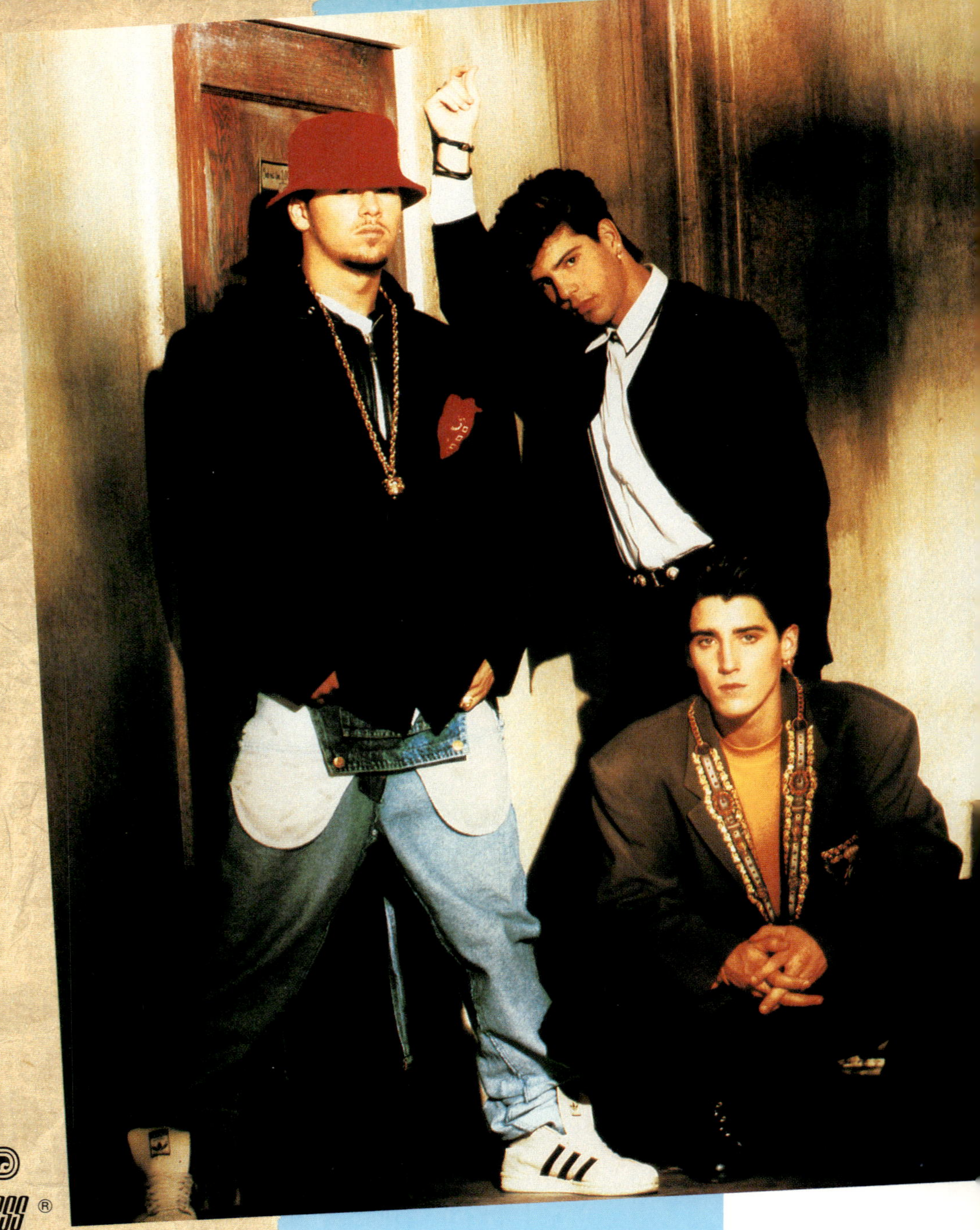

CONTENTS

38	. . . FACTFILE ON JOSEPH
40	. . . COMPETITION WINNERS
41	. . . WIN A GOLD DISC!
43	. . . SCRAPBOOK 4
45	. . . JONATHAN PROFILE
46	. . . NEW DISCS ON THE BLOCK
48	. . . NKOTB FAN CLUB
52	. . . FACTFILE ON DONNIE
57	. . . DANNY PROFILE
58	. . . JOSEPH PROFILE
59	. . . ANSWERS PAGE, SCRAPBOOK 5
61	. . . GOODBYE . . . UNTIL THE NEXT TIME

Written by Tommy Jay with additional material by Kim Glover.
Edited by Dick Wallis, Century 22 Ltd.
Designed by Marc Abbott & Stuart Young.
Photographs by Lynn Goldsmith, L.G.I.
Published in Great Britain by World International Publishing Ltd.,
an Egmont Company,
Egmont House,
P.O. Box 111, Great Ducie Street,
Manchester M60 3BL.
Printed in Great Britain. ISBN 0 7498 0401 7.

THE NEW KIDS

On Saturday April 20 1991, the NEW KIDS ON THE BLOCK arrived in Berlin, Germany to start the European leg of their tour. It had all been kept very quiet so that there would be no fuss at the airport but somehow – surprise, surprise – many of their fans and friends had found out the time of arrival (MI5 eat your heart out!), and were there to welcome the guys in the usual way. Donnie, Jonathan, Jordan, Danny and Joseph were surprised but more than a little pleased to see everybody. After a day's relaxation the tour started in the DEUTSCHLANDHALLE in Berlin to tumultuous applause. The whole place was charged with excitement as the German fans welcomed the idols they had been waiting to see for so long. Several more German cities were to come under the NEW KIDS spell and then they were on to Sweden, Belgium, France, Switzerland and Holland before the UK. The guys slipped into the UK via Dover, having crossed the channel by ferry and for once confusing many fans who laid siege to Heathrow airport sure in the knowledge that Donnie, Jonathan, Jordan, Danny and Joseph along with their entourage would arrive in England there. When the NEW KIDS found out

OVER EUROPE

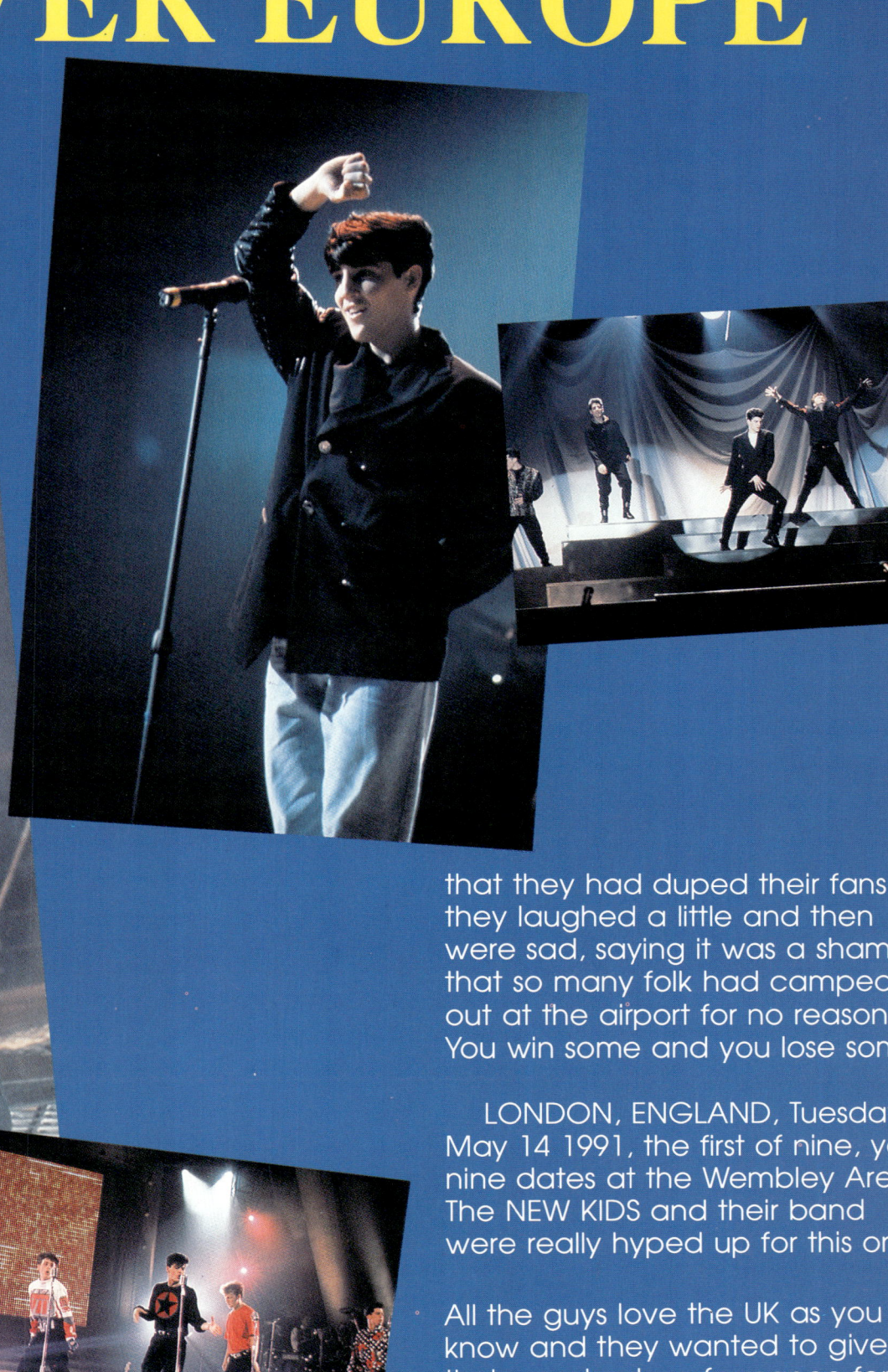

that they had duped their fans they laughed a little and then were sad, saying it was a shame that so many folk had camped out at the airport for no reason. You win some and you lose some!

LONDON, ENGLAND, Tuesday May 14 1991, the first of nine, yes nine dates at the Wembley Arena. The NEW KIDS and their band were really hyped up for this one.

All the guys love the UK as you know and they wanted to give their very best performance for everyone. Just before showtime, the atmosphere back-stage was

stretched taut as a tightrope. All of the KIDS were more nervous than usual, laughing and joking with each other. The crowd was going wild with anticipation and when the guys finally made it on to the stage, the welcome which they received was quite literally deafening. Dancing and singing brilliantly the NEW KIDS led the crowd through the show, winding them up, bringing them down, winding them up a little more and then, with each and every fan more in love with them than ever, they launched into the finale. Scenes of mayhem follow the guys off stage with thousands of fans trying to catch a last glimpse of their favourite KIDS. Back to the hotel, and, guess what, the NEW KID secret service has been working overtime and three or four hundred fans are waiting outside. "We love you! Welcome to London!" is heard between bouts of screaming and chanting as Donnie, Jonathan, Jordan, Danny and Joseph make their way into the hotel, exhausted but elated by the reception that London had given them once again. Everyone loves the NEW KIDS and what's really cool is that they try to do as many things as possible for folk that are somewhat less fortunate than themselves. Before every gig they have special fans back-stage to meet and chat with them. There are many photo albums around the world with pictures of stunned fans staring incredulously at a NEW KID. As many of you will know it was Danny and Jordan's

birthdays during their first week in London. A secret birthday party was planned and they had a great time partying with their families and friends.

At Birmingham NEC for five shows and then to the final shows in London – throughout the whole of the tour the fans were fantastic. On many occasions faces appeared that were recognised from other gigs in Europe and quite a few of you went to every show in the UK just to hang around outside the venue or hotel with the hope that one of the KIDS would catch your eye and talk to you, give you an autograph and have a picture taken! You're all totally MAD! but every single NEW KID thinks the world of you.

Joseph graduated whilst in London and his brother brought over his graduation papers as a surprise. Other members of Joseph's family were already in London and they all joined together in celebration. Whilst on tour there are often fairly long periods of inactivity and to combat this Donnie, Jonathan, Jordan, Danny and Joseph along with certain members of their management and crew would head for a basketball court. Some serious games were played in an atmosphere of friendly competition. The guys are all pretty good players and like to keep their hand in, even on their travels.

June 1 1991. Not only is this the last night in the UK, but it's also the last night of touring for a few months. Something special had to happen as the NEW KIDS were all going off in different directions for a very well-earned vacation. Behind the scenes it was just like school breaking up, everyone being just a little silly, including the KIDS. Showtime was bound to be different and so it proved – Donnie, Jonathan, Jordan, Danny and Joseph had what amounts to a huge party on stage. It was nothing like one of their normal

shows, but still equally as exciting. Throughout the night a constant stream of friends joined the NEW KIDS on stage in various mad-cap antics and the whole thing climaxed with crew, family and friends all up on stage. An enormous explosion brought the final curtain down on what had been a hectic and tiring, but hugely enjoyable tour. Breaking down the show for the last time on this tour the crew said their goodbyes to the KIDS and their families and many a tear was shed. The frivolity and antics carried on back at the hotel deep into the night but even though everyone had fun, the occasion was tinged with sadness. For the next day Donnie, Jonathan, Jordan, Danny and Joseph, their management, families and crew would be boarding the big metal bird and heading homeward to the USA. Tired, but elated the NEW KIDS will be taking a break from touring but will soon be rehearsing a new show that could be back on the road by November '91. So, watch this space!

STAGE NAME:
JORDAN

Full Name: Jordan Nathaniel Marcel Knight
Nickname: "J"

BASIC STATS:
Birthday: May 17, 1970

Birth Sign: Taurus
Home: Boston, Massachusetts
Weight: 155-160 lbs - It depends (11 st 1-6 lbs
Height: 5' 11"
Eye Colour: Brown
Hair Colour: Brown

FAMILY INFO:
Parents: Marlene Putman and Allan Knight
Brothers and Sisters: Allison, Sharon, David, Christopher, Jonathan
Nephews: Matthew, Robert, Nathaniel
Nieces: Alicia, Justine
School and Grade: English High - Graduated

FAVOURITE THINGS:
Car: Don't know. Don't really care
Male Singer: Luther Vandross, Michael Jackson
Group: The Stylistics
Movie: The Godfather, The Untouchables
Drink: Milk
Food: Lasagne
Own Record: I'll Be Lovin' You Forever and Baby, I Believe In You
Subject in School: English, social issues, music
Sport: Basketball, ping-pong, swimming
Sports Team: Celtics
Hobbies: Reading, swimming
Biggest Turn-on: People being nice to others
Biggest Turn-off: People acting like jerks to others because they're different
Goals: To be happy in whatever I do
Message to Fans: Thank you for everything you've done, for being so loyal, for touching my heart. I am forever grateful
Qualities in a Friend: Someone who won't pressure you into doing something you don't want to do
Most Prized Possession: My family

Jordan

Jordan

"Fame, Yo! I love it."

"Sure we should all do our bit for peace and ecology. We got to live here too don't we?"

"The worst thing about being a NEW KID is the lack of privacy."

"Our fans do some crazy things. One actually telephones my dentist masquerading as my mother to find out what time I should arrive for an appointment, so she can meet me there. Luckily, my dentist manages to see through her wheeze."

Donnie

"Peace and love, it's the only way."

"Me, outspoken? Yeah, I guess I can be."

"It's a real emotional experience for me when I go on stage. Sometimes it's so beautiful it brings tears to my eyes."

"Sometimes I scare myself."

"We ain't saints, just positive people."

"Fans are always after our autographs, but sometimes we are rushing from one place to another so we don't have time to sign any. They're all pretty cool about it though, they know we sign as many as we can."

eighteen

N WORDS . . .

Joseph

"Nervous? Sure, we all still get nervous before a show, it gives you an edge."

"At last people really do seem to be thinking about the planet."

"We sometimes laugh a lot at what we read in the papers and magazines. It would seem that the press know more about us than we do!"

"It's a hard life on the road, but I pretty much enjoy it most of the time."

Danny

"The NEW KIDS, the band and the crew, it's got to be one of the biggest families ever."

"Eat healthy, stay healthy. You are what you eat."

"Sometimes our tour manager Cathy has one heck of a job keeping us in check, but we love her."

Jonathan

"Fame won't change the way real friends treat you."

"I quite often get asked, 'Do fans bother me?' The answer is NO! I knew what I was getting into and we all love them."

"I just love to be out in the countryside among the sights and sounds of nature."

"A holiday? Yeah, great, we need one!"

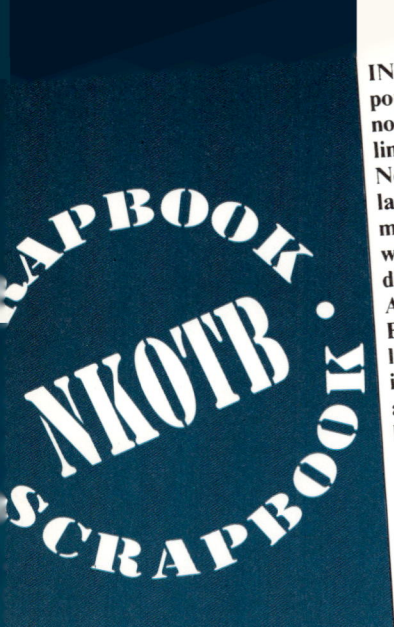

Rock and Pop

IN the fickle world of pop music teen sensations normally have a very limited shelf life, and when New Kids On The Block last toured the UK many music critics wondered when the hysteria would die down for the five young Americans.

But instead of disappearing like so many teenybop idols before them, the Kids are back playing to packed houses throughout Europe. At the Wembley Arena last week the air was shrill with the sounds of whistles and screams as the excitement reached fever pitch even before Danny, Joe, Jordan, Jonathan and Donnie took to the stage. With a small tight backing band featuring two keyboards, guitar, bass and drums they rattled through their run of top ten hits. Maybe not everything was in tune but their choreography and dance routines put some of today's rap acts to shame. They are a disciplined pop act at the top of their particular tree and will probably still be performing when they are Old Kids and the screamers have kids of their own.

Front row rating: 8 out of 10

SENSATIONAL: New Kids On The Block

THEY'RE KID-CRAZY!

By DAVID HANCOCK

SCREAMING girls besieged a top hotel yesterday desperate for a glimpse of their pop idols, New Kids on the Block.

Police had to put up barriers as hundreds turned up outside London's Mayfair Hotel.

And one youngster ended up a Kid Nicked on the Block when she ignored warnings to stay off the road.

Two burly cops finally pounced and hauled her off to a police van.

Another five were also held for "running in and out of the traffic."

The kids begin a sell-out tour at Wembley tonight. They will travel in three blacked-out Renault B110 vans nicknamed the "tanks."

The £30,000 luxurious vans are equipped with TVs, videos, CD players, coffee machines and telephones.

Girls storm a top hotel

SCREAMING: Fans waiting for a glimpse of their idols

BLUB! BLUB!

The **New Kids** were most upset not to be at the awards ceremony. Unfortunately, they had to be on stage that night! They collected their award a few days later at BBC TV Centre, minutes before their mega-brill live appearance on *Top Of The Pops*.

STAGE NAME: DANNY (DAVE)
Full Name: Daniel W. Wood
Nickname: None

BASIC STATS:
Birthday: May 14, 1969
Birth Sign: Taurus
Home: Boston, Massachusetts
Weight: 160 lbs (11 st 6 lbs)
Height: 5' 7½"
Eye Colour: Brown
Hair Colour: Black

FAMILY INFO:
Parents: Daniel and Elizabeth Wood
Brothers and Sisters: Bethany, Melissa, Pam, Brett, Rachel
Niece: Daniela

FAVOURITE THINGS:
Car: Jeeps and trucks
Male Singer: Lots
Female Singer: Patti LaBelle
Group: Lots
Movie: Star Wars series
TV Show: Don't watch too much TV
Food: Good food
Fast Food: None
Snacks: Popcorn
Drink: Water
Own Record: Games
Subject in School: Maths
Sport: Basketball
Sports Team: Celtics, Red Sox
Hobbies: Relaxing, exercising
Biggest Turn-on: Kind and caring
Biggest Turn-off: A pushy know-it-all
Goals: To become a producer or writer
Message to Fans: Hold on to your dreams, don't believe the hype
Qualities in a Friend: Trustworthy. Friendship means the most
Most Prized Possession: Gold and platinum records
Qualities in a Girlfriend: Kind, caring, a friend, warm, cute, compassionate

Everything you needed to know . . .

Once the KIDS got to a hotel and found that some girls had rearranged the booking of their rooms so they were not on a private floor, but their floor!

The Knight family have had to build a 6' fence around their house to keep out the FANS!

Jordan once went downstairs in his house to get some water at 3am and a fan was waiting in the garden and snapped him through the window.

Danny has been asked to write a book on keep fit!

Jordan loves basket ball.

Joe's very favourite guy is Ol' Blue Eyes himself, Frank Sinatra.

Danny worked as a cook in the early NEW KID days.

Jordan Knight is the tallest NEW KID at 5' 11".

A girl once got to the front of the stage in a special place designated for wheelchairs – she then jumped out of the chair and grabbed Donnie – she had used the wheelchair as a ruse to get to the front!

Donnie used to work in a bank.

Jonathan Knight used to work in a pizza restaurant.

Jordan used to work at a summer camp.

All the KIDS love to skateboard, the only problem is they *all* think they're the best!

Danny says he'll eat anything once, his Mom always used to say "Try it! You may even like it!"

Joseph was once asked for his autograph in a toilet – the girl just walked in!

Jonathan was once spotted by FANS in the hotel jacuzzi. TRICKY!

Jon loves his teddy bears. He has around 5,000.

Jordan and Donnie once disguised themselves as hot dog vendors. Good idea, eh? Yup, but it only worked for 10 minutes!

Donnie says one of the best things about being famous is thousands of girls asking for *your* autograph. What more could a guy ask for?

twenty seven

NEW KIDS QUIZ

1) Who has just graduated?

2) Who is Marlene?

3) Donnie is involved with one of his brothers in another musical project. What is its name?

4) What was May 14 1969?

5) What are the NEW KIDS' star signs?

6) The NEW KIDS' first ever single was called?

7) Who is a shopaholic?

8) Who loves computer games?

9) Who's the heart-throb of the group?

10) The healthiest NEW KID (he thinks!)?

11) Who supports Boston Celtics?

Answers on page 59

GIANT NEW KIDS WORD SEARCH

Use your skill to find 8 things connected with the NEW KIDS in the word search below.

```
W O P A I J T N O W P Z Y W B C G
I D F S Z D O N N I E O U M O S R
L I T K L E D I S A B O R R R E I
I C K T H A Y I N C K T A C C R D
T E H I E T R M E T I O A K E C L
B D A Y V U S M E A D O C I D C E
E I I Q D R S H N E D O N A D P Y
S Z S U Z A A N E Z O R A L E F O
A X I E M A N D E B T D E N Y I U
M M Y S M I K I O U N H Y A I O R
E E N E W K Z I R C V S A E B A B
B J O L Z I O I C U I F O A D L E
O S Q L N Y M C U V F O E S C O R
R E E K E F D K T Q X L H I B B H
E C L V L F D P C O D E L D A K S
D A N U F D P C O S E P L N D E A
G M E P L S J O S R O U B W I W D
L E A D S E T T L O W E L Y G I S
K I L P L L E T T S L E R N E W A
R O U A N D B H T L E R N E W A S
S M X P L Z S O B A K H A W K I D
```

Donnie   Boston

Jonathan   Dick Scott

Jordan   New Kids On the Block

Danny   Joseph

Answers on page 59

Danny performs a breakdancing routine with Jordan. In Germany Jordan tried to caterpillar across the stage – but Joe ran out and sat on him!

new kids on the block
LIVE
IN BRITAIN
AN 8-PAGE SOUVENIR OF THEIR 1991 TO...

People are comparing Jordan to a young George Michael. He has slight stubble and performs songs with a very soulful voice.

The stage set is much bigger than last time. It boasts a wall of eight 7ft speakers and 12 sets of lasers each costing £3,000. Five men sit up in the roof of the stage set and control the lights.

The only New Kid who has all his food especially flown in is Danny, because of his strict body building diet. He needs special high-protein foods to keep his muscles looking good!

Joe has got really big over the last year – he's grown another couple of inches. He now wears his hair slicked back and slinky leather trousers. He also performs a heavy metal version of Treat Me Right.

Donnie, however, still looks like a ragamuffin. Donnie's the only New Kid who chooses his own stage clothes. During the show he wears his black dungarees (which he's recently cut down) with hobnail boots and a baseball cap. He also wears his skeleton jeans as seen on the No More Games sleeve. The costume changes during the show are really fast!

During the show the Kids have a habit of running into the audience, much to the annoyance of their many minders!

Jonathan

STAGE NAME:
JONATHAN

Full Name: Jonathan Rashleigh Knight
Nickname: None

BASIC STATS:
Birthday: November 29, 1968
Birth Sign: Sagittarius
Home: Boston, Massachusetts
Weight: 155 lbs (11 st 1 lb)
Height: 5' 11"
Eye Colour: Hazel
Hair Colour: Brown

FAMILY INFO:
Parents: Marlene Putman and Allan Knight
Brothers and Sisters: Allison, Sharon, David, Christopher, Jordan
Nephews: Matthew, Robert, Nathaniel
Nieces: Alicia, Justine
School and Grade: Graduated High School

FAVOURITE THINGS:
Car: Anything with four wheels and an engine
Movie: No time to have a favourite anymore
TV Show: No time to have a favourite anymore
Food: Italian or Mom's home cooking
Fast Food: Burgers and fries
Snacks: Chocolate
Subject in School: Science
Sport: Water Sports
Sports Team: Celtics, Red Sox, Patriots, Bruins
Hobbies: Shopping
Biggest Turn-on: Health, happiness, peace
Biggest Turn-off: War, pollution, racism
Goals: To be as good as I can in what I pursue
Message to Fans: Be the best you can be, be yourself
Qualities in a Friend: Honest, fun
Most Prized Possession: Health, career

HOW TO HANG AROUND AN AIRPORT WITH
NEW KIDS ON THE BLOCK!

SCRAPBOOK · NKOTB · SCRAPBOOK · SCRAPBOOK

1. Wait patiently until your boarding gate number appears on the little computer thingy attached to a wall, pillar or other such piece of brickwork and look exceedingly bored in the meantime!

2. Until then it's often a good idea to grab a drink and a bite to eat before boarding your plane as you can never be sure of what edible surprises the stewardess will throw in your direction!

3. Once aboard the plane spread yourself over several seats and pretend that you're not really a New Kid by hiding under your snazzy leather jacket!

4. Assist your fellow New Kids in their air-bound slumber by bringing them pillows on which to rest their weary heads.

5. And then scarper as quickly as possible once you've landed!

Joe decided he wanted to wish Jordan a happy birthday in an unforgettable way!

Joe's handiwork in all its glory!

Jordan sits surrounded by cards and pressies in his £250 a night room at the Mayfair Hotel. The New Kids and their crew had nearly a whole floor of the hotel to themselves!

Jordan nipped out through the hotel's kitchen to get to his party and avoid being mobbed!

Biscuit, the New Kids' former minder, was one of the special guests at Jordan's party

Jordan is 'Mr Show Business'. He lives and breathes music, it is part of his very soul. Drawing inspiration from almost any source of stimulation he will write a new melody or dream up a dance routine for a NEW KIDS show by imagining it in his head, so he can sometimes appear to be in another world. Although when first meeting him he may come across as a little shy, he is in fact a very strong character and can be quite tough and brave. Somewhat more rebellious than his elder brother Jonathan, he's the strong silent type, but is very adaptable and will make the best of almost every situation, generally seeing the funny side of things. Jordan has become quite a dab hand at using disguises and often helps the other NEW KIDS when they feel the need to 'disappear'. He has a formidable collection of props to choose from, but he's able to improvise should it be necessary, seeing a disguise in almost everything that's wearable. If you have a problem with any electrical gadget, Jordan's your man. He has a mysterious talent that enables him to mend broken things as if by magic. He's not particularly technically minded, but a wiggle here and a thump or tap there will nearly always make the offending item come to life again. Definitely the 'true romantic' of the band he will pick a flower and give it to a pretty fan or quote poetry (the romantic type) for her or some other kind words if she looks like she needs cheering up. His stunning good looks qualify him most definitely as the band's heart-throb.

Donnie Wahlberg

Donnie is to all intents and purposes what can only be called a rock'n'roll activist. He is the NEW KID with a mission, any cause that he has an affinity with he will uphold with all his heart. One of his main hates is injustice, he will often put himself on the line to right a wrong. The rebellious one of the group, Donnie sees his position as a means which allows him to state his point of view and he will take advantage of all the resources available to him to this end. He has a lot to say for himself on many of the social problems that afflict our society today, conducting himself clearly and with an impressive knowledge of matters. You could never call Donnie subtle, to him a situation is never out of his control, and to prove it he'll always come up with another wild idea on the spur of the moment.

Spontaneous, full of energy, even hyper are words which spring to mind when trying to describe him. He has a heart of gold underneath that slightly daunting exterior. His family and friends mean everything to him, but he expects the most from people and will be very hurt if someone lets him down. He comes across initially as a little scary but make friends with Donnie and you'll have a friend for life and he'll keep you in fits with his wacky sense of humour. He loves to play jokes on the other guys and sometimes they will say that he is completely mad. Just be warned however, he can be quite a toughie.

Joseph

STAGE NAME:
JOSEPH McINTYRE

Full Name: Joseph Mulrey McIntyre
Nickname: Joey Joe

BASiC STATS:
Birthday: December 31, 1972
Birth Sign: Capricorn
Home: Boston, believe it!
Weight: 145 lbs (10 st 5 lbs)
Height: 5' 8"
Eye Colour: Blue
Hair Colour: Brown

FAMILY INFO:
Parents: Katherine and Thomas McIntyre
Brothers and Sisters: Judy, Alice, Susan, Tricia, Carol, Jean, Kate, Tommy
Niece: Kayla
School and Grade: Catholic Memorial, 12th

FAVOURITE THINGS:
Car: Sidekick
Male Singer: Frank Sinatra
Female Singer: Madonna
Group: The McIntyre Girls!
Movie: Midnight Run, Godfather I and II
TV Show: 20/20
Drink: Soda water with lime
Food: Mama's meatloaf
Fast Food: Burgers
Snacks: Lemonade, Gatorade and Hot Tamales
Author: Judy McIntyre (playwright)
Book: Chocolate War
Own Record: Call It What You Want
Subject in School: U.S. History
Sport: Football
Sports Team: Boston Celtics
Hobbies: Chillin' with the fellas!
Biggest Turn-on: Being home and happy
Biggest Turn-off: People misunderstanding me and all those stupid lies
Goals: To be a good person, to be happy and to live forever large
Message to Fans: Thank you for taking me where I am today. I love you!
Qualities in a Friend: I have three best friends – Tom, Paul, Jon! Quality in friends is thinking alike
Most Prized Possession: My family
Qualities in a Girlfriend: Logic, looks, lovable, long lasting

WIN A GO

This is an original Platinum Disc presented to NEW KIDS ON THE BLOCK for sales of more than 300,000 copies of **Hangin' Tough. Step By Step** has now gone gold and you can win an exclusive **Step By Step** Gold Disc personally inscribed with your name.

All you have to do to enter is write a 5-line limerick about one of your Favourite Five, using one of these first lines to start you off. The best five limericks will each win a Gold Disc.

1. Donnie is a rebel . . .
2. Jonathan can be quiet . . .
3. Jordan is so dishy . . .
4. Danny, he's the dancer . . .
5. Joseph is so cute . . .

Entries must be in by 31st January 1992, so get rhymin' and remember KEEP IT CLEAN!

Send your limerick, stating your full name, address and age to: NEW KIDS ON THE BLOCK GOLD DISC COMPETITION, Editorial Department, World International Publishing, Egmont House, PO Box 111, Great Ducie Street, Manchester M60 3BL.

Last year's Drawing Competition had a fantastic response. There are some chillin' artists out there and here are the two winners.

Age group 5-10 years Claire Richardson, Chaddesden, Derby.

Age group 11-16 years Sonja Szvetecz, Oberiexingen, Germany.

OLD DISC!

be won in this fabulous competition!

Gina 16, Kerry 16, Samantha 16, Dawn 16, Sarah 16
Samantha: "We've been here for three days and I've touched three of them, ahhh! We've tried to get in the hotel once but we got caught at the deliveries door. The guards told us that we'd be arrested if we went near. It's a 99 per cent chance that you'll never see leave, but we don't care. It's a 99 per cent chance that you'll never see them, so you have to take the risk."

Here's the most unsecretive, secret hide-out of the New Kids. Just think, they're in there somewhere, ahhhhh!

Sevian 14, Nancy 13, Caroline 14, Charlotte 15, Asha 16

Asha: "I'm from Leicester and came up on my own three days ago. I've been sleeping at the front of the hotel and last night I got to see them so it was all worth it."

Charlotte: "I shoved Joe out of the way today cos I thought he was a bodyguard. I was trying to get a picture of Danny — I almost went mad! I've tried to sneak up the fire escape a few times but I keep getting caught."

Lizzy 14, Bridget 14, Maria 14, Fiona 14
Fiona: "We couldn't go to school today because we got a letter saying that it was too unhygenic — honest! We've tried to break into the hotel four times and have got caught twice. When I got in once, I tried to get into the laundry basket but I was spotted."

I've seen all of them today except for Jon. I liked ... e at the beginning because of his gorgeous blue eyes, ... n I liked Donny because of his strong personality, but now I just think they're both horny!"

Dionne 19

And All Because They Love...NKOTB!

They're completely loopy! Absolutely raving bonkers! They hide in laundry baskets, get chased out of buildings and scale perilous fire escapes. Who? The New Kids' adoring fans of course! Number One trotted along to NKOTB's hideaway in London, The Mayfair Hotel, to ask the trillions of fans camped outside what they'd do to see their idols!

Shoppa 14
"I came on my own because my other friends went to school. I'm missing drama and science but I can catch up quickly. I've already tried to book a room under another name, but you have to leave a £500 deposit first! I did manage to sneak into the hotel and hide in the toilets for a while; they're absolutely huge with suites and chandeliers — the toilets are nicer than my bedroom!"

Donna: "We didn't go to school because New Kids are more important! My mum brought us down from Cirencester for the concert and we're going back tonight. We tried to get in through the restaurant door before, but everyone just stared at us so we ran away."

Joan: "The girls were so keen to see them that I thought I'd join them. I have to like them I suppose; I haven't heard anything of theirs I don't like, so I'm looking forward to the show."

Rebecca: "We've tried to get in the hotel hundreds of times but we keep getting caught. All we want is to see them to have just one kiss — then maybe a few more, ha ha!"

Sally 14, Kelly 15, Sam 14, Katrina 15, Pippa 16, Rebecca 14, Eisha 15, Theresa 15

Jonathan Knight

Jonathan is 'big brother' to the band. He is a bit of a worrier and needs to know what is going on at all times. He could easily be called the watch-dog of the group as he is very concerned with all aspects of the group's business affairs and takes a very active interest in them. Ambitious and decisive he is known in the group as a take charge kind of guy but actually he is doing it in the best interests of the NEW KIDS. He will tell you that he loves privacy, but in truth he is no loner and likes to feel the security of people around him. A shopaholic, he likes nothing better than wandering around a store looking for something to add to his already massive wardrobe. Probably the most fashion conscious of the NEW KIDS, Jonathan has the most amazing collection of leather jackets which is staggering in itself. He is organised beyond belief, analytical and logical. He is the guy that the NEW KIDS will come to for advice on business or career problems and he'll help usually with very sound comments backed up with flow charts, graphs, diagrams and the like. He can be a little sensitive sometimes, not knowing which way to take a prank that he has just become the butt of, but will generally laugh. He is a sucker for really dumb jokes and funny faces and can be seen physically trying not to laugh because he has a very loud, wild laugh. Both Donnie and Joseph know exactly how to make him crack up. When he does succumb, a really childlike, carefree side of him is released and he will laugh for hours. Jonathan is an avid animal lover and would like nothing better than to surround himself with dogs, cats and horses, something he intends to do in the future. He already has one dog. Home is a very special place for Jonathan, and his family are very important to him. It will be a very, very lucky girl that ties this guy down.

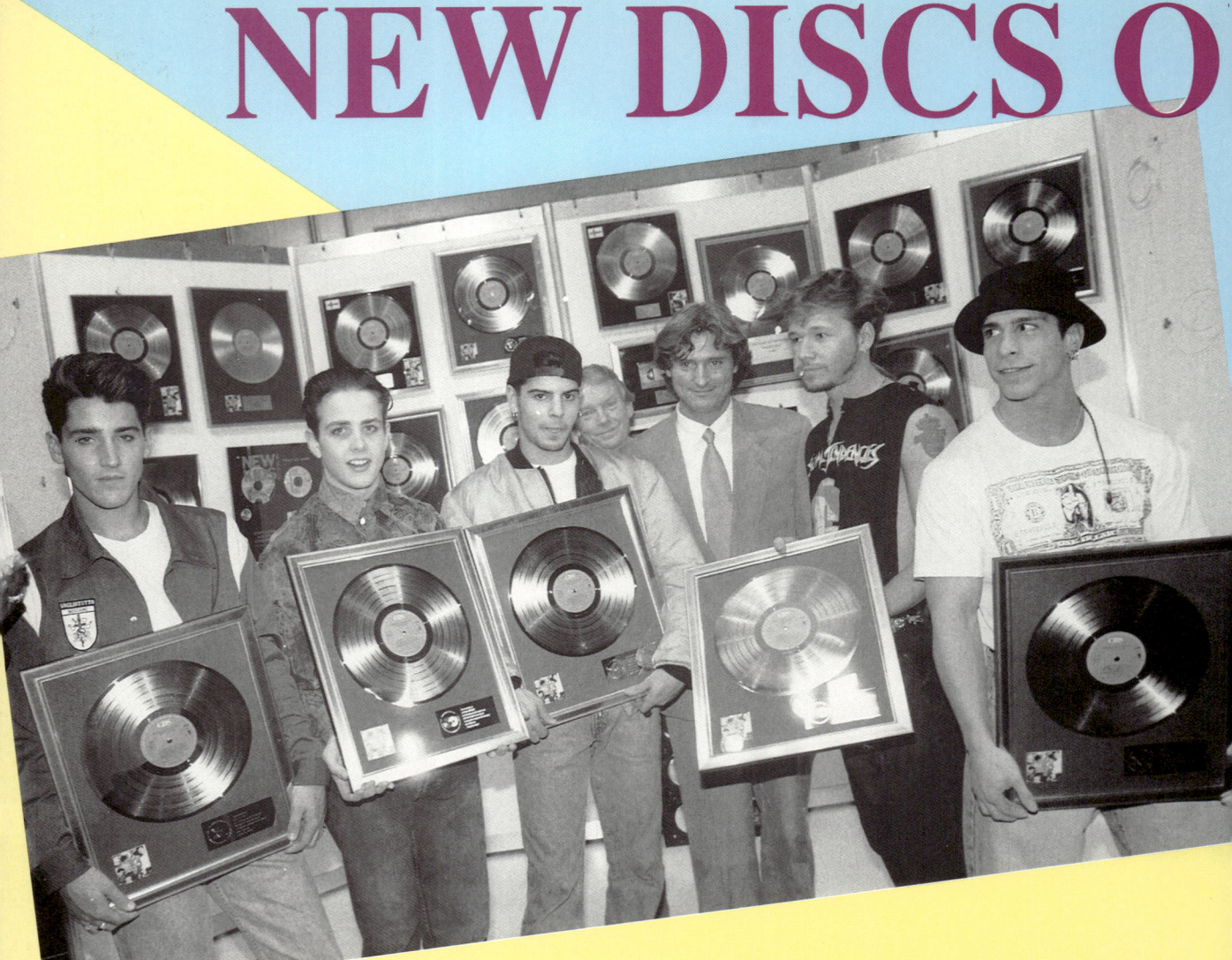

It was an extraordinary sight – five NEW KIDS and countless Gold, Platinum and Silver Discs! The occasion? A special presentation by Sony to the NEW KIDS ON THE BLOCK of loads of accumulated awards from all their European record companies.

They all got together at the Intercontinental Hotel in Berlin on April 22 before the opening date of the No Games Tour. As you can see, there was quite a celebration and it was all to mark mammoth sales of NEW KIDS records throughout Europe. Due to the varying sizes of different countries the number of records you have to sell to get a Platinum Disc varies from country to country as you'll see from the table.

That's an awful lot of discs to carry home, but you can be sure the KIDS will be back for more!

THE BLOCK!

COUNTRY	ALBUM	STATUS/SALES REQUIREMENT	
GERMANY	STEP BY STEP	PLATINUM	(500,000)
SPAIN	HANGIN' TOUGH	GOLD	(50,000)
	STEP BY STEP	PLATINUM	(100,000)
	NO MORE GAMES	PLATINUM	(100,000)
FRANCE	STEP BY STEP	PLATINUM	(300,000)
SWITZERLAND	STEP BY STEP	GOLD	(25,000)
FINLAND	HANGIN' TOUGH	GOLD	(25,000)
	STEP BY STEP	GOLD	(25,000)
AUSTRIA	HANGIN' TOUGH	GOLD	(25,000)
	STEP BY STEP	GOLD	(25,000)
SWEDEN	STEP BY STEP	GOLD	(50,000)
HOLLAND	STEP BY STEP	GOLD	(50,000)
BELGIUM	STEP BY STEP	GOLD	(25,000)
NORWAY	HANGIN' TOUGH	SILVER	(25,000)
	STEP BY STEP	SILVER	(25,000)

NEW KIDS ON THE BLOCK™ OFFICIAL INTERNATIONAL FAN CLUB

If you would like to keep in touch with what's happening to the NEW KIDS ON THE BLOCK, why not join the Official International Fan Club? You'll receive a great membership pack, including a club badge, your very own membership card as well as group and individual photos of the NEW KIDS. You will also get a quarterly newsletter with lots of information about what the NEW KIDS have been getting up to, along with hot info on record and video releases and tour dates. To join, just fill in the form below – if you don't want to damage your book just copy the relevant details onto a sheet of paper – and send it with your yearly subscription of £10.00 to:-

NEW KIDS ON THE BLOCK OFFICIAL INTERNATIONAL FAN CLUB
PO Box 79, Ashford, Kent, TN23 3AG.

NEW KIDS ON THE BLOCK™ OFFICIAL INTERNATIONAL FAN CLUB

I wish to join the NEW KIDS ON THE BLOCK™ OFFICIAL INTERNATIONAL FAN CLUB.

.... and I am .... years old.

My name is ....
....

I live at
....
.... Postcode
....
....

I enclose my cheque\postal order for £10.00 (ten pounds) as my yearly subscription and I look forward to receiving my membership pack for which I understand I have to allow up to 28 days for delivery. PLEASE DO NOT SEND CASH in the mail – cheques or postal orders only.

Thank you.

forty nine

FAVOURITE THINGS:

Car: None
Male Singer: Arron Hall (Guy), Chuck D. (Rapper), Jordan Knight and Bobby Brown
Female Singer: Depends on mood
Group: Public Enemy
Movie: Sometimes Scarface, sometimes Midnight Run, sometimes another movie
TV Show: None
Drink: Water
Food: Depends on my mood, I always enjoy home cooking
Fast Food: Depends on my mood
Snacks: Depends on my mood
Book: Autobiography of Malcolm X
Own Record: Depends on my mood
Subject in School: Maths, it almost always has a solution
Sport: Baseball
Sports Team: All home teams of Boston
Hobbies: Too many to name – no lie
Biggest Turn-on: Being turned on and learning something new
Biggest Turn-off: Being turned off
Goals: To live to see the day when this country lives up to its reputation
Message to Fans: Try not to judge things till you've been educated on them
Qualities in a Friend: Open-mindedness is my o... credential
Most Prized Possession: My brain and my far...

STAGE NAME:
DONNIE WAHLBERG

Full Name: Donald E. Wahlberg
Nickname: Cheese

BASIC STATS:
Birthday: August 17, 1969
Birth Sign: Leo
Home: Dorchester, Massachusetts
Weight: 155 lbs (11 st 1 lb)
Height: 5' 10"
Eye Colour: Hazel
Hair Colour: Blonde

FAMILY INFO:
Parents: Alma and Donnie Wahlberg Sr.
Brothers and Sisters: Mark, Bobbo, Jimbo, Paul, Arthur, Michelle, Tracey, Debbie
Nephews: Brandon (Buster), Adam (Prince), Donnie (Baby "D")
School and Grade: Graduated, but always learning

Donnie

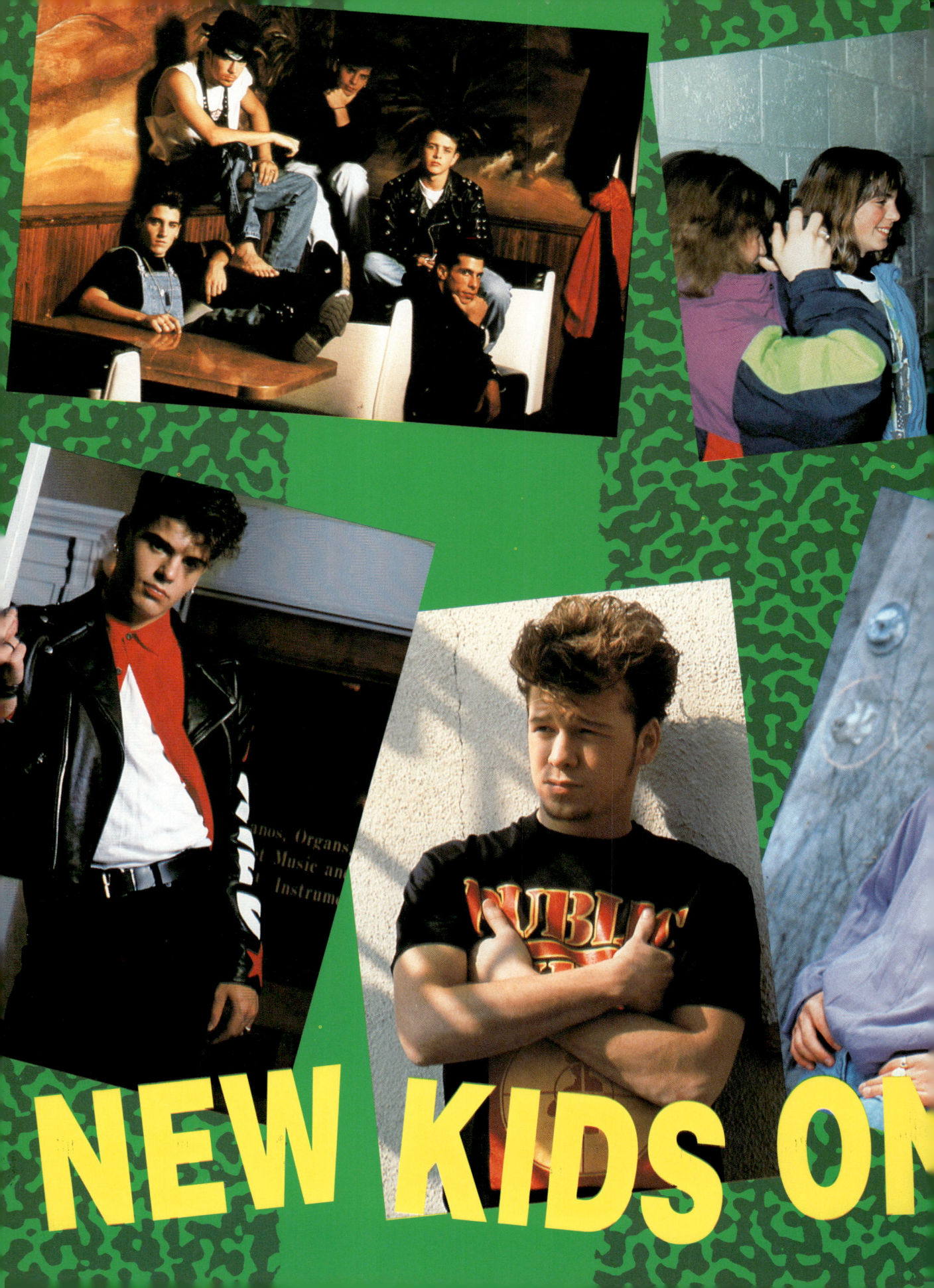

NEW KIDS ON

THE BLOCK!

Danny is probably the most easy-going of the NEW KIDS. He is always optimistic and cheerful no matter what the situation. A confirmed health food freak and body-builder, he is quite muscular and easily the most athletic KID. This is not to say that the others are lacking in fitness, but with Danny, being fit takes on an almost religious fanaticism. An exceptional dancer he has the grace of a natural athlete and the poise of one who knows he is in control of his body. Sometimes a little stubborn and set in his ways, but with a really good sense of humour, his general demeanour is pretty stable and he would love to be everybody's best friend. He's the guy that all the NEW KIDS can talk to about a problem they might have and he's always the one to renew flagging spirits in the band (sure it happens sometimes) if it is necessary and can always be relied upon to whip up one of his healthy concoctions to help an ailing NEW KID recover, though sometimes the thought of taking the mixture (tofu and seaweed milk shake!) is medicine enough. Seriously though, Danny is a veritable boffin on the subject of healthy living, so much so that he has been asked to write a book on the subject, which he intends to do in the very near future. Always the helpful one but quite dogmatic, if a job needs doing he'll not waver from the task but he'll take the simplest and most straightforward route to achieve a conclusion. He'd be a good person to have around the house as he is very practical and good with his hands, but he might cause a few grey hairs as he is very self-critical. If he put a shelf up and it wasn't quite right (although you probably wouldn't notice) he'd be just as likely to pull it all down and start again. Kind, considerate and very faithful he loves his home, loves to please people and he has the most wonderful smile which spreads right across his face and could melt ice with its warmth. A real nice guy.

Joseph McIntyre

Joseph will tell you that he is sick of being called a 'KID', quite rightly so as he has grown into a really good-looking young man over the past few years. He still has an air of innocence about him which belies the pranks and practical jokes he gets up to, the other NEW KIDS and their crew usually being the target. He is a natural performer and has been working as an artist from a very early age. On stage he is theatrical and dramatic, if sometimes just a little flashy, and the fans adore him. When he locks eyes with them the words he utters are for their ears only. He loves Frank Sinatra and would love to follow in his idol's footsteps. He is working really hard with his vocal coach on his technique to perfect that already fabulous voice, with the hope of one day fulfilling this dream. Joseph is a winner and a very competitive person, but is basically very sweet-natured and would never do somebody down just to come first. He wouldn't hurt a fly. He loves life to be an adventure and if he wasn't a NEW KID he'd probably have some really dangerous occupation, a test pilot or an astronaut or something along the lines of 'Indiana Jones'. However, he'll be the first to tell you that he loves what he does and intends to enjoy it to the hilt. He has a wild unbounded imagination and a wicked, mischievous twinkle in his blue eyes which often means trouble for the other guys. Like Jordan he loves disguises and will quite often masquerade as the bell boy in a hotel or a room service waiter, many times fooling the rest of the gang although they are becoming wise to him now! Joseph also has a social conscience which Donnie is fuelling. He's quite a complex character but can get away with almost anything by reverting to being everyone's little brother and putting on his innocent 'who me?' face. He has become a very confident young man and will no doubt achieve most of his ambitions by just being Joseph.

Teen-dreams: Jim White reviews New Kids on the Block

Hey, kids, rock 'n' roll!

GLYNN GRIFFITHS

Because they are no longer kids, New Kids On The Block now like to call themselves NKOTB. At first glance, the post-item to be announcing the arrival of a group called KNOB. It is appropriate mishearing. New Kids are the latest in a line which stretches back to the Beatles, back Elvis, back to Frank Sinatra even; the honourable heritage of satisfying teenage girls' burgeoning sexual fantasies. Judging by the way some of the forward little things at Wembley reacted every time a Kid thrust his groin in their direction, the Kids do it rather well.

12,000 pubescent girls in emotional turmoil is an extraordinary thing to witness. Fifteen minutes before lights down an announcement that the concert was about to begin sent them scuttling back from the hot dog, coke and popcorn stands like over-excited rabbits. Once in their places they took photos of each other cuddling the souvenir programme (£8) or waved the fluorescent headbands (£3) they had just bought from a canny Arena entrepreneur. Crescendos of screaming would erupt for unlikely reasons: when a children's television presenter took his seat, when the record on the PA system, when the girl next to you started.

As the lights finally dimmed the noise from the ranks of referee's whistles and over-developed larynxes made Motorhead seem decibel-shy. Insensitive to changes in pace or tone (ballads, rockers and raps received the same high-pitched response) it was a noise that could perforate car-drums at 200 paces. It assaulted the fore-head, the back of the neck, the armpits. And, for two hours, it did not stop.

When the five Kids finally emerged from the gloaming, at a stroke doubling the number of boys in the Arena, the noise made it almost impossible to decipher what (or indeed whether) they were singing. So you had to watch instead.

Theirs was an energetic performance, choreographed but not slick. They seemed rather uneasy with their syncopated dance routines (the Jackson Five they aren't) preferring the bits when they could prance around, with much hip-hop finger pointing, making the most of a stage crammed with walkways and platforms. Behind them a small but competent band did their best not to provide any visual distrac-tions, a humility eschewed by a light show which over-dosed on pyrotechnics.

After almost every song, often in the middle of songs, there was some scripted rabble-rousing de-signed to push the screaming off the Richter Scale. "It gets kinda lonely on the road," one of them said. "And I've been looking for that one special girl."

"I'm here," bawled the 11 year old in front of me, with the cycling shorts, the puppy fat and the bum-bag full of sweets. She meant it.

In fact, like everyone there, she loved every mo-ment of it. "Check this out," Donnie said at one

point. "We have been right across the country of Eu-rope. Sorry, the continent of Europe. But we just could not wait 'til we were in London, England." It was, you won't be surprised to hear, because the best audiences in the world were to be found in London, England. Which might come as a surprise to those who had recently been told they hailed from Frank-furt, Germany or Paris, France or Helsinki, Finland.

It appears that New Kids like to offer all things to all men (or rather girls). They do not have a homoge-nous image: Jordan is a slick crooner, Danny a would-be B-Boy, Donnie a dirty rebel, the other two

New Kids on the Block: 'They seemed rather uneasy with their syncopated dance routines, preferring the bits when they could prance around'

not much of anything. And their music is a hybrid of rock, pop, soul, hip-hop, reggae dancehall, even Beatles pastiche. On paper it works a mess, but in execution it works because someone has thought it through.

The genius behind New Kids is called Maurice Starr, who should write a book on teenage psychol-ogy. He invented them after he found that New Edition, a teenage vocal group he put together in the early Eighties failed to capture the worldwide market. They were good, but they were black. So he reckoned a teenage vocal group where white would crack it. He was right.

But it takes time for the hype to percolate. When New Kids first appeared in Britain at the Smash Hits concert in November 1989 the audience looked on blankly, unim-pressed. They were waiting for Bros to appear.

However, once the momentum began it was unstoppable. And Starr has controlled it brilliantly, subtly repositioning the Kids im-age from clean boys with teeth to naughty bad boys with stubble. Mirroring the business relation-ship, everything is tightly re-hearsed on stage. Nothing is out of place. When Donnie lashes out and sends a mike stand flying, the spot light is perfectly positioned to catch this spontaneous act of re-bellious violence.

Starr knows how to milk an au-dience, and these boys are not bad conduits for his talent. But, Jor-dan's decent voice notwithstand-ing, it is only Donnie who you would bet on to make it without his svengali.

While it is unlikely Melvyn Bragg will devote a South Bank Show to him in a later incarnation, Donnie has presence. He is a star, despite flashing the waistband of his Y-fronts during frequent periods of chest baring, he wears the baseball cap – with a healthy swagger. Attain-able, rebellious, an unthreatening bit of rough, he is the perfect teen sex symbol. If you were an 11-year-old girl, you would fancy him.

Outside, two of the massed ranks of mums waiting to drive their exhausted daughters home appeared not to agree. They were loudly discussing how pop had gone down hill since they were kids. When Donny Osmond and David Cassidy ruled the world

1) The ultimate New Kids fan, page 18
2) Further gig details below

Fans greet idols with Berlin wall of screams

From DAVID HANCOCK in Berlin

HEIL, heil rock 'n' roll. The screams of German weenybop-pers built up into a Berlin wall of sound to welcome New Kids On The Block back on the road in Europe.

Fans from both sides of the formerly divided city swarmed together and shouted themselves hoarse as they waited for Boston's famous five to hit the stage.

Then, like New Kids lovers everywhere, they showered their idols with a barrage of teddy bears.

The first struck Donnie Wahlberg's shoulder. The second got Joe McIntyre in the stomach. And so many furry toys rained down that minders were forced to sweep them back into the audience.

A year ago Danny Wood slipped on one and sprained his ankle and had to quit the group's British tour. Since then the New Kids have pulled in another £200 million - including a sizeable chunk for being in TV's latest Coke ad.

But the constant touring that has put them at the top of pop's big earners is in danger of taking its toll.

The New Kids had no time to rehearse a new show. So on the current tour, No More Games, their act is barely different from last year's.

Dancing

And occasionally the dancing that was the group's hallmark looks more lacklustre than superstellar.

But none of that mattered to the 5,000 Blockhead fans many of them pre-teenage girls, as they pushed forward inside the giant German arena to try to touch their heroes.

"Jordan, Jordan," 11-year-old Freda Krefeld screamed at Jordan Knight before flinging her arms around her friend and sobbing.

Her friend carried an English-language placard declaring "Joe Is Sexy." Both girls were from the East side of Berlin and a little over a year ago could only dream of being at such a show.

Bouncers carried out faint-ing girls over the heads of others to the front of the stage for treatment.

Girls too hoarse to scream any more stood with glazed stares.

Similar scenes in London and Birmingham next month

Around 150,000 British fans will queue not only to see New Kids but to buy the expensive merchan-dise that is also making the group a fortune.

In Berlin tickets cost £13 programmes were £7 a time with T-shirts at £8 and sweatshirts at £20.

Dreams

Like the Germans first-ish fans want to see lead singer Jordan in red shirt and black trousers danc-ing during Call It What You Want.

And the sight of Jo McIntyre in in black leathers will figure in dreams for months.

Bad boy Donnie who avoided all over a hotel fire will send fans frantic as he rips off his shirt in Hank Tonk.

New Kids will even tually have to choose their act to stay ahead of the competition.

But come next month's British tour, there'll still be plenty of ordinary kids on the block screaming for tickets.

SINGING OUT: Lead vocalist Jordan in the spotlight with the microphone

BARING UP: Heartthrob Do

Pictures CHRIS GRIEVE

We have to go now (have to get back to lying in the sun, ha-ha!). Seriously folks, we're gonna be back in harness real soon, putting together a whole new show for you to see when we start touring again, so life will get hectic pretty soon.

All of us are really looking forward to seeing all our old friends, and making lots of new ones, and it goes without saying that we love you all.

Each and every one of you is really special to us.

Take Care

Love and Peace